Fairness

By Bruce S. Glassman

With an Introduction by
Michael Josephson,
Founder of CHARACTER COUNTS!_{SM}

JOSEPHSON INSTITUTE
INSTITUTE
CHARACTERCOUNTS!

JOSEPHSON
INSTITUTE
CHARACTERCOUNTS!

Produced and created in partnership with Josephson Institute

Special Thanks goes to the following people, whose help on this project was invaluable:

At CHARACTER COUNTS!:
Michael Josephson
Rich Jarc
Amanda Skinner
Mimi Drop
Michelle Del Castillo

Content Advisers:
Dave Bender, book publisher
Tracy Hughes, educator
& CHARACTER COUNTS!
coordinator for Meadowbrook
Middle School, San Diego
Cindy De Clercq, Elementary
School Principal

And thanks to:
Nathan Glassman-Hughes,
Emma Glassman-Hughes,
Natalia Mata, Erica Warren,
Ebony Sanders, Kellen
O'Connell, Nicole Rigler,
and Alex Olberding

Library of Congress Cataloging-in-Publication Data

Glassman, Bruce.
Fairness / written by Bruce S. Glassman. — 1st ed.
p. cm. — (Six Pillars of Character series)
Includes bibliographical references and index.
ISBN-13: 978-1-60108-504-7 (hardcover); ISBN-10: 1-60108-504-4 (hardcover)
ISBN-13: 978-1-60108-505-4 (pbk.); ISBN-10: 1-60108-505-2 (pbk.)
1. Fairness—Juvenile literature. I. Title.

BJ1533.F2G53 2009
179'.9—dc22   2008001125
Printed in China

Contents

Thinking About Character

By Michael Josephson, Founder, CHARACTER COUNTS!

magine that you're taking a big test at the end of the year. You really want to do well on it. You're stuck on a few questions—answers you know will make the difference between a good grade and a possible poor grade. You look up from your test and realize that you can clearly read the answers from the student sitting next to you. You're now faced with a choice. Do you copy the answers or do you go back to staring at your own sheet?

You consider the choices. You know that, if you cheat, you probably won't get caught. And, you think to yourself, copying a few answers is relatively harmless. Who does it hurt? And, besides, everyone does it, right?

Every day you are faced with choices that test your character.

So, what do you do?

Your honest answer to this question will tell you a great deal about your character. Your answer reflects not only what you know is right and wrong, but also how you *act* with what you know.

You are faced with important choices every day. Some choices are "preference choices"—for example, what to wear to school, what to buy for lunch, or what to buy your dad for his birthday. Other choices are "ethical choices." These choices are about what's right and wrong. These are the choices that reflect character.

Ethics play a part in more daily decisions than you may think. The test-taking scenario is only one example of an ethical choice.

You are faced with ethical choices every day. One of the main goals of this series is to show you how to recognize which choices are ethical choices. Another main goal is to show you how to make the right ethical choices.

About Being Ethical

Being ethical isn't simply about what is allowed—or legal—and what is not. You can often find a legal way to do what is unethical. Maybe you saw that a cashier at the grocery store forgot to ring up one of your items. There is no law that says you must tell him or her. But, is it ethical to just walk out without mentioning it? The answer is no. You're still being dishonest by taking something you did not pay for.

So, being ethical is about something more than "what you can get away with." It is about what you do because *you know it's the right thing to do*—regardless of who's watching and regardless of whether you may stand to gain. Often there is a price to pay for doing the right thing.

Character Takes Courage

There are many obstacles to being ethical—chances are you're faced with some of them every day. Maybe you don't want to be

There are many obstacles to being ethical. Overcoming them takes courage and hard work.

embarrassed by telling the truth. Or maybe you feel doing the right thing will take too much effort. Few good things come without a cost. Becoming a person of character is hard work. Here is a poem I wrote that makes this point.

It's Not Easy

Let's be honest. Ethics is not for wimps.

It's not easy being a good person.

It's not easy to be honest when it might be costly, to play fair when others cheat or to keep inconvenient promises.

It's not easy to stand up for our beliefs and still respect differing viewpoints.

It's not easy to control powerful impulses, to be accountable for our attitudes and actions, to tackle unpleasant tasks or to sacrifice the now for later.

It's not easy to bear criticism and learn from it without getting angry, to take advice or to admit error.

It's not easy to really feel genuine remorse and apologize sincerely, or to accept an apology graciously and truly forgive.

It's not easy to stop feeling like a victim, to resist cynicism and to make the best of every situation.

It's not easy to be consistently kind, to think of others first, to judge generously, to give the benefit of the doubt.

It's not easy to be grateful or to give without concern for reward or gratitude.

It's not easy to fail and still keep trying, to learn from failure, to risk failing again, to start over, to lose with grace or to be glad for the success of another.

It's not easy to avoid excuses and rationalizations or to resist temptations.

No, being a person of character is not easy.

That's why it's such a lofty goal and an admirable achievement.

Character Is Worth It!

I sincerely hope that you will learn and use the ideas of CHARACTER COUNTS! The books in this series will show you the core values (the Six Pillars) of good character. These values will help you in all aspects of your life—and for many years to come. I encourage you to use these ideas as a kind of "guide-rail" on your journey to adulthood. With "guide-rails," your journey is more likely to bring you to a place where you can be a truly good, happy, and ethical person.

Michael Josephson
Founder of Josephson Institute and CHARACTER COUNTS!

What Is Fairness?

When we talk about fairness, we are really talking about justice, too. Most people think of fairness as part of personal relationships and situations of everyday life. For example, if you are given chores to do around the house, it's only fair that your siblings get chores, too.

We tend to think of justice as a bigger kind of fairness. It is a fairness that applies to society and even to the entire world. Justice is what we get from our legal system. It comes from a complicated process that (we believe) is designed to be the most fair to the most people most of the time.

**Justice comes from our legal system—
it is how we apply fairness to our society.**

Learning how to be fair can often take a lifetime.

To be a person of good character you must know how to be fair with others. This is something that must be learned. Most people spend a lifetime working at it. Good character also requires that you make sure others are fair to you, and also to others you know.

Process and Consequences

When we look at a decision, we consider two main things to determine fairness. The first is how the decision was made, or the process used to consider the options. The second thing is the consequence of the decision itself.

For us to consider a decision to be fair, we must know the process, or method, used in the decision-making. If we don't believe the process was fair, we won't believe the decision was fair, either. For example, you may get a homework assignment back from your teacher graded with a "B" (or two stars out of three). You will likely accept that grade, knowing that your teacher is a fair and consistent person. But what if you found out that, this time, your teacher used a coin toss to determine who got two stars and who got three? Would you feel the grade was fair once you knew how it was determined?

The second part of considering a decision to be fair is to judge the consequence of it. A consistent process may be used, but it may yield a result that is not fair. For example, a decision may benefit one person more than it should. Or it may have too big a negative effect. Lawyers and judges spend a good deal of time debating and appealing decisions that were made in a court of law. Often, an appeal is made because—even though a verdict was reached with a fair process—it yielded a result that was unfair.

If a verdict—or decision—seems unfair, it may be appealed and brought back to court.

What's a Fair Process?

Being fair takes a lot of time and effort. It means considering things carefully. It also means considering all sides of an issue, without a predetermined opinion or preference.

A truly fair process usually includes four key things: Fair notice, impartiality (no preference for the outcome), gathering of all the facts, and fair hearing. Let's look at what each of these things means.

Fair Notice

Before a person's conduct can be considered wrong, a person must know it is wrong and do it anyway. Consider this example:

> *Ashlee just transferred from Sycamore Middle School to Bryant Middle School. Today is her first day at Bryant. She wants to make a good impression, so she dresses in her favorite outfit and her favorite cap.*
>
> *When Ashlee shows up for her first class, she is immediately sent to the assistant principal's office. When she asks why, the teacher says that wearing caps violates the Bryant school dress code. When she arrives at the office, Ashlee explains that the Sycamore dress code allowed caps. It didn't occur to her that Bryant would not allow them.*

What do you think the assistant principal should do? Should Ashlee be punished just like any other student for violating dress code?

The fair decision would be to give Ashlee a pass this time. She didn't know all the rules at her new school. She hadn't had fair notice.

What do you think the assistant principal should do if Ashlee shows up the next day wearing a cap?

Impartiality

The term *impartiality* means not having a preference for one outcome over another. It means not pre-judging. If you need a decision to be made or a dispute to be resolved, you want to be confident that the person or people deciding are impartial. For example, would you rather have a dispute with your friend settled by your friend's brother or by another person who is unrelated? Chances are you'd prefer the unrelated person. That's because you know it would be hard for the brother to be completely impartial.

Being impartial is the most important ability a judge must have.

Seating an Impartial Jury

In the American legal system, many trials are decided by a jury. The most important requirement for any jury is that it be impartial. So, how do juries get selected? It is a somewhat lengthy and time-consuming process.

First, a group of people are selected randomly—usually by a computer. That group becomes the possible jury pool. People in the jury pool sit down with the lawyers and the judge in the case. The judge and lawyers then ask many questions of the potential jurors. In legal language, this process is called *voir dire.* The term is Anglo-French and means "to speak the truth."

People in the jury pool are asked about their background, life experi-

Selecting jurors who can be fair is one of the most important parts of any trial.

ences, and opinions. The judge and lawyers listen carefully to the answers. They need to determine which people can weigh the evidence of the specific case most fairly and objectively. For example, a defendant may be on trial for drunk driving. The judge and lawyers would likely ask if any of the potential jurors has ever been arrested for drunk driving. They may ask if anyone has a relative who was arrested for drunk driving. They may ask if anyone is a police officer, or is related to a police officer. They may even ask if anyone has a financial interest in any alcohol-related business. After hearing the answers to these and many other questions, the judge and the lawyers will decide if they feel any of the potential jurors cannot be impartial in the case. Those people will be dismissed from the case.

Through *voir dire*, an attorney can also use a limited number of "peremptory" challenges to dismiss potential jurors. No specific reason is required for these dismissals.

Those individuals who are accepted by both attorneys and the trial judge are sworn in as the jury.

Complete and absolute impartiality is, of course, impossible to achieve. The many layers in the jury selection process, however, insure that each jury has the greatest level of impartiality possible from the group of potential jurors.

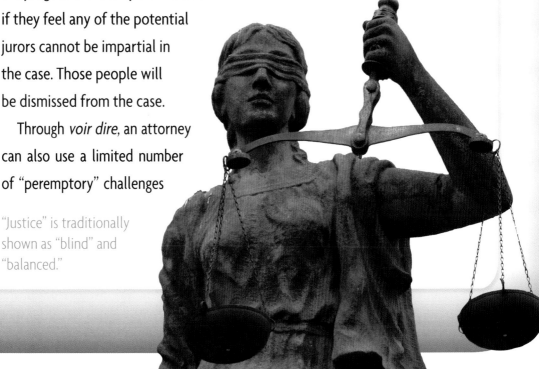

"Justice" is traditionally shown as "blind" and "balanced."

Being impartial is not easy. It requires a great deal of honesty and self-awareness. It also requires patience and self-control. We all have opinions, preferences, and prejudices in certain areas. Sometimes, we are aware of what those prejudices are. Other times we are not. And sometimes we are aware, but we refuse to admit to them.

Gathering All of the Facts

This piece of the fairness process is about making sure all important information has been gathered before any decision is made. It means that both—or all—sides of a story are available. It means that the circumstances of an event or issue are as clear as possible. It also means that no relevant details or facts are left out or are kept from anyone.

An important part of being fair is remembering that there often is more than one side to a story. That means, you should always be careful to hear another person's point of view before making a judgment. This is not only true in a court of law. This sort of fairness is also a big part of personal relationships. Communication plays a key role here. With communication, you

Communication is key to being fair with others in your personal relationships.

understand what someone else was thinking, or what she was feeling. Most of the time, understanding the needs and feelings of others makes a lot of things clear. It also allows you to be fair by really listening to all the facts.

Another key piece of gathering all the facts is determining intent. The idea of intent is one of the most important concepts in our legal system. Intention is doing something on purpose. When deciding a case, a judge and jury must figure out if a crime was intentional. The answer makes a big difference in what the consequences are. For example, there's a big difference legally between accidently hitting someone with a car and trying to run them over.

Determining intention and gathering facts is another important part of being fair in personal relationships as well. If you're like most people, you assume you know the intentions of others much of the time. But, often, what we think we know is different from what is actually true. Communication, gathering the facts, and listening to others will reveal feelings and motives you may not have known before. Consider this story:

> *Margie and Dina had recently become the best of friends. They wanted to spend as much time together as possible. After school on Friday, Dina told Margie she would call on Saturday morning to plan their time together.*

On Saturday morning, Margie kept her cell phone in her hand, waiting for it to ring. Noon came and went, but there was no call. Then it was 2:00 in the afternoon, and still Dina had not called. The longer she waited, the more hurt Margie felt. She was convinced that Dina didn't care about her any more. Or that she had found a better best friend.

On Monday morning, Margie ran up to Dina, who turned away. When Margie asked why Dina didn't return her calls, Dina turned around in surprise. "Your calls?" she said angrily. "I never got any calls!"

"Well, I called you, like six times on Saturday morning, just like I said I would," Margie explained. "Maybe there's something wrong with your phone."

Dina whipped out her cell phone and flipped it open. Then she saw. The phone was dead. She had forgotten to charge the battery. She turned to Margie. "Ya know what, Marge? I feel really dumb. I *thought you were blowing me off. I was convinced we weren't friends any more. I guess I should have waited to get all the facts before I made a judgment like that."*

"You bet!" said Dina. "You're my best friend. I would never do something like that to you. Next time, plug that thing in, will ya?"

The girls shared a big laugh and went off arm-in-arm to their first class.

Have you ever had someone assume something about you that wasn't true? Or assume you had certain intentions that you didn't? How did it feel?

Have you ever made snap judgments about someone else?

Fair Hearing

The final piece of the fairness process is about making sure everyone involved in an issue has a fair chance to tell their side of a story. Just as gathering all the facts is important, so is hearing everyone's opinion or version of events.

A fair hearing involves listening with an open mind. It also involves giving everyone an equal opportunity to be heard. It is helpful to remember another key idea that comes from the American legal system.

To be fair, you need to listen to the facts with an open mind and not assume from the beginning that someone else is wrong.

It says that a person is "innocent until proven guilty."

When you first hear the facts, it may be hard to remain convinced of someone's innocence. Fairness requires, however, that you avoid judgment until the very end.

Fairness and Consequences

We have looked at the importance of fairness in thinking about decisions. The process of how we go about making a decision must be impartial, complete, and fair to all. But there is another part we must look at. When we look at fairness and decision-making, we must also look at the fairness of the decision itself.

Every decision has some result, or consequence. To be fair, we must make sure the consequences are the most fair to the most people. We must also be sure that consequence is fitting for the issue at hand. In legal terms, this is known as "just punishment." For example, it means you shouldn't get a life sentence in jail as punishment for J-walking.

There are a few things to remember when thinking about the fairness of decisions. The first is that, no matter what the decision, there will likely be some people who feel it is unfair. Generally, those who feel like the "winners" in a decision will think it is fair. Those who feel like the losers in a decision will think of it as unjust.

The second thing to remember about a decision is that it should be defensible. That means, there should be a good explanation of how the decision was reached—and why the decision was made the way it was. This is why a fair process is so important. If you always use a fair process, you will most often get a fair result.

No matter what the decision, it is likely some will feel it is unjust.

Can a Fair Process Fail?

In 1692, some people in Salem, Massachusetts were accused of being witches.

The idea of what is fair can change. Most of the time, we consider "fair" to mean whatever most people in our society agree is fair. But different people in different societies agree on different standards of fairness. And people in different times have had different standards of fairness.

In Salem, Massachusetts, in 1692, for example, people were tried in a courtroom for being witches. The process of the trial was accepted by the majority as being fair, even though it involved all kinds of cruel treatment. Often, accusations were made that could never be proved. Looking back on those trials today, we consider them to be terribly unfair.

Our world today is changing very fast. Every day, advances in technology, science, and medicine make previously unimagined things possible.

Science and technology can also change what we consider to be fair. The science of DNA testing, for example, has changed the course of justice in America's legal system.

DNA is genetic material found in every human being. And everyone's DNA is unique—like a fingerprint. There is DNA in hair, fingernails, even saliva. Before DNA testing was available, many people were convicted of crimes based on all the other evidence. They were given "fair" trials, using the best process available. When DNA tests became possible, however, the definition of a "fair process" changed. DNA evidence can now prove or disprove guilt more reliably than anything else.

DNA evidence has freed about 140 people who were wrongly convicted of crimes and imprisoned. Twelve of those prisoners had been sentenced to death. Now, DNA evidence is a key element in any trial we consider to be "fair."

In January 2008, DNA evidence freed Tim Masters, who had been wrongly convicted of murder. He had spent 10 years in jail.

chapter 2

The Importance of Fairness

Fairness is important to everyone. The desire to be treated fairly is one of the most basic desires all human beings have. In order to strive for something, a person must know he has a fair chance to get it.

Countless battles throughout history have been fought by people who desired fairness and justice. Many of those battles have been fought on battlefields, with actual weapons. Many others have been fought in courtrooms and government buildings by people armed with knowledge and the force of their arguments.

Benjamin Franklin, John Adams, and Thomas Jefferson work on a draft of the Declaration. America's Founders were determined to make fairness a key element of the new government.

Some of America's greatest achievements have been the result of a battle for equality, fairness, and justice. The American Revolution, for example, began as a protest against unfair taxes.

The Civil War was fueled, in part, by a conflict between America's North and South over slavery. Many people in the North felt slavery was unjust. Many in the South, for whom slavery was a part of every-day life, felt slavery was fair.

In 1920, the Nineteenth Amendment to the Constitution finally gave American women the right to vote. That amendment was the result of decades of struggle and protest by brave leaders such as Elizabeth Cady Stanton and Susan B. Anthony.

Suffragists (women who fought for the right to vote) spent nearly 100 years protesting unfair laws before they won their battle.

Martin Luther King, Jr. was a leader in the struggle to end the unfair practice of segregation in America.

In 1964, President Lyndon Johnson signed the Civil Rights Act. This finally outlawed segregation (dividing people by race) in schools and public places. That law came about due to the countless civil rights protests that had been organized by Dr. Martin Luther King, Jr. and other African-American leaders. Those brave people dedicated their lives to securing equality for all Americans, regardless of race.

Fairness in Sports History

As long as there have been sports, there have been controversies over fairness. No matter what the sport, or the era in which it is played, there have been people willing to cheat in order to win. Sometimes they cheat by using different equipment. Other times they cheat by trickery or stealing information from an opponent. Recently, much of the focus on cheating has been centered on the use of banned substances in sports.

Most sports organizations—amateur or professional—have a list of substances that are illegal for athletes to take. Most of these lists forbid stimulants, which boost energy. Also banned are steroids, which artificially promote large muscle growth, among other things.

For many years, the biggest scandal in Major League Baseball has focused on steroid use. Some superstar players, such as Jose Canseco, have admitted to using steroids. Canseco has said that he knows many players who also use steroids and other illegal drugs.

By far the biggest steroid controversy in baseball has been centered on Barry Bonds. Many people are convinced that Bonds has taken steroids to build his muscles and increase his strength. Those people point out how Bonds grew so much bigger over the years. Despite all the controversy, Bonds never failed a test for illegal substances. In the meantime, he has been hounded by the media. And he was forced to live every moment of his public life as if he had already been found guilty.

In November 2007, Bonds was indicted (called to court) to answer charges that he lied about steroid use. Before he ever showed up in court, however, many people had already made up their minds. They were sure Bonds was guilty.

So why do so many people care about this one baseball player? Well, a large number of people feel that Barry Bonds may be the greatest player ever to play the game. The question is: Is he still the greatest player of all time if he accomplished what he did while on steroids?

Here is a summary of Bonds's baseball accomplishments, as of 2007:

1. He holds the all-time Major League Baseball home-run record with 762. On August 7, 2007, he broke the previous record of 755, set by Hank Aaron.

2. He is the all-time career leader in walks (2,558) and intentional walks (688).

3. He holds the Major League record for single-season home runs, 73.

4. He has been awarded MVP a record seven times, and has received four of those in consecutive years—also a record.

5. He has won 8 Golden Gloves.

6. He holds a place in the standings for many other hitting records, some for which only baseball legends such as Babe Ruth and Lou Gehrig stand in his way.

Before Barry Bonds ever showed up in court, many people had decided for themselves that he was guilty.

Here are some of the issues that make up the Barry Bonds debate. They may help you decide what you think about the issue.

Some people say that steroids have made Bonds the star that he is. Others say that, even if he did take the drugs (which is yet to be proved), they didn't give him the playing skills he has shown. As Boston Red Sox slugger David Ortiz once said, whether you take steroids or not, "you still have to swing the bat."

Some people say you cannot compare present-day players to players from long ago. Today, athletes have access to better training, more nutritional options, and improved playing equipment, such as bats, gloves,

In 2007, Barry Bonds broke Hank Aaron's all-time home run record.

and balls. Others say that records are made to be broken. If players today can train better, then they simply become better players than those in the past.

When Bonds hit his record-breaking home-run in San Francisco in 2007, the ball was caught by a 21-year-old student from New York City. It was eventually sold at auction to fashion designer Marc Ecko for $752,467. Ecko set up a web site so the American people could decide what happened to the historic ball.

When all the votes were in, the fans had decided to send the ball to Cooperstown with an asterisk. The asterisk would denote the controversy surrounding Bonds and steroids. Ecko said that the fans's decision showed that "this was shrouded in a chapter of baseball history that wasn't necessarily the clearest it could be."

The reaction to the decision was mixed. The Hall of Fame said it was "delighted to have the ball." Many players and managers in Major League Baseball felt that the Hall of Fame was disrespecting Bonds by accepting the ball.

Bonds himself said that, if the ball was put on display with the asterisk, he would boycott the Hall of Fame. That means, he would not attend the ceremony if and when he was inducted.

Consider all these issues. What do you think is fair? How should the record and the baseball be treated? And how do you think the amazing career of Barry Bonds should be listed in the history books?

chapter 3

Fairness in Your Life

The basic idea of fairness is relatively simple. We all understand what it means. Everyone wants to be treated fairly. But putting fairness into everyday practice is not so easy. It takes discipline and self-control. Being truly fair means being consistent—making similar decisions in the same way all the time. It means being impartial—not allowing your personal beliefs to affect how you treat others. It also means being honest in all you do.

People can be consistent and impartial without using the exact same standards for being fair. Different people have different ideas of what fairness should be based on. Here are six different common ideas about how to decide what is fair:

Playing sports is one way we learn to be fair, consistent, and honest.

The Theory of Merit

This is the idea that people are entitled to whatever they can get based on their skill, talent, or hard work. Those people who do not have the skills or who do not work hard are not "entitled" to be given anything. This idea does not mean that people who "have" should not give to those who don't. Charity and caring about those who are less fortunate should be part of everyone's life. But, strictly in terms of fairness, the idea of merit is based on earning what you get.

For many people, a fair society provides basic human needs to all its members.

The Theory of Need

This idea says that all people are entitled to certain basic things—for example, the basic human needs of food, shelter, and clothing. This theory also says that it is the responsibility of a just and fair society to provide all its members with their basic needs.

The Theory of Might

This is the idea that power should determine who gets what. It says that a person is entitled to whatever they can get, regardless of merit, need, effort, or skill. This is also known as the theory of "might makes right."

The Theory of Equality

This theory says that every person is entitled to an equal share of whatever is available, regardless of merit, effort, need, skill, or might. This theory reflects a belief that it is unfair for some people to have a great deal more than others, even if some have "earned it" and others have not.

The Theory of Seniority

This idea gives preference to those who have "been around" the longest. It gives "credit" for work and achievements that have been done in the past. For example, if two players on the soccer team break the same rule, the coach might go easier on the player who has been on the team for three years, over the player who just joined last week.

The Theory of Effort

With this model, a person is entitled to benefits that reflect how much effort he or she expends. These benefits are given regardless of merit, need, skill, or other factors. This is the idea that people should be rewarded for trying hard, no matter what the actual result of their effort is.

What do you think is the most fair theory?

As you read before, understanding fairness is much easier than putting it into practice. As you get older, you will need to use your ability to be fair more and more. And you will need to be able to judge the fairness of others.

Here is a situation for you to consider. It will help you think about fairness in your everyday life. It will help you think about what your standards of fairness are. It will also help you think about how you can go about making difficult decisions fairly.

Imagine that you just won five tickets to go see the hottest rock concert of the year (they're front row seats and come with a backstage pass!). When you make a list of all the people you should invite, you come up with five. That means someone has to be cut off the list. Here is a description of each person:

Cameron is your newest best friend. Over the past three months you've spent the most time together. You happen to know this band is Cameron's all-time favorite and he would do anything to get a ticket.

Tammy has been an okay friend for four years. She has invited you to every birthday party and special event she's had over the years. You know she really likes this band and could never afford to go on her own.

Taylor is your oldest friend. Though you've grown apart recently, it's a longstanding tradition that you always invite each other to birthdays and special events. You happen to know that Taylor doesn't really care all that much about this particular band.

Pat plays in your band has been a good friend for a while. Pat has the best attitude and would be the most fun to have along.

Your cousin Kris is going to be a guest at your house the week of the concert. You're not that close, but Kris is your age and really likes rock music.

One of these people can't come. There are many things to consider. And many possible outcomes. There is no single right answer. How will you go about making that decision? How will you decide what is fair?

How you decide the questions above will tell you a good deal about how you make choices. Making good choices is probably the single most important thing you can do in life. Good choices lead to good outcomes. And good outcomes lead to happiness and success. Learning how to make good choices is relatively easy. Actually making the good choices in real life is the hard part.

Learning How to Make Good Choices

William Jennings Bryan

A famous lawyer and speechmaker named William Jennings Bryan once said, "Destiny is not a matter of chance, it is a matter of choice." He was saying that we have more control over our lives than we often assume.

More than anything else, your life will be affected by the choices you make. Knowing how to make good choices is most often the difference between being happy and being miserable.

Two Core Principles of Choice-Making

There are two fundamental principles that form the foundation of good decision-making. They are:

1. We all have the power to decide what we do and what we say.
2. We are morally responsible for the consequences of our choices.

The first principle goes back to what William Jennings Bryan said: your destiny is your choice. But what about when you feel powerless and out of control? We all feel this way at times—especially kids and teens.

It's important to remember that having the power to make choices doesn't mean you have to make every choice alone. You also have the power to seek out good advice and to get the counsel of people you trust. So, part of making good choices is knowing how to get the help you need to make them.

The second principle is about understanding the full impact of the decisions you make. Every choice has a consequence—whether good or bad. And every choice affects certain people in some way. The people that are affected by a given choice are called "stakeholders." Most of us never even realize how many stakeholders there are for a given choice. Have you ever copied songs from a friend onto your MP3 player? Can you think of all the stakeholders affected by that choice? (Hint: It's not just you and the friend you copied from. Start

One Person Cheats, Everyone Loses

In October 2007, gold-medalist runner Marion Jones made a startling admission. She admitted that she used steroids while competing in the 2000 Olympics in Sydney, Australia. Steroids are a banned substance for

Marion Jones crosses the finish line to win the gold medal in the 100-meter race at the 2000 Olympics.

Olympic athletes. Jones's confession meant that her records would be stricken and her medals would be taken away.

At the Sydney Olympics, Jones won three gold medals and two bronze medals. One of the golds and one of the bronzes were from relay races. Because Jones was part of those races, her teammates were also forced to give up their medals.

All in all, eight teammates were directly affected by what Jones did. Indirectly, all the Olympic runners from Sydney—in fact all the athletes of the world—were affected. Without Jones competing, the outcomes of those races could have been completely different. Olympic Chairman Peter Ueberroth said, "It's very unfortunate, but your

Jones cries as she explains to reporters that she lied about using performance-enhancing drugs.

result involved cheating, so the result is unfair to the other athletes of the world."

In his closing remarks, Ueberroth assured sports fans everywhere. He said, "We have a responsibility to compete fairly. That's our system, and that's the way we're going to live."

Seeking good advice from people you trust is key to making sound decisions.

thinking about the music download service, and the employees at the record company that sells the songs, and the musicians, producers, and engineers that work to create each song...).

So, thinking about all the stakeholders in a decision is one way to consider how important that decision is. It's another way of saying that the greater the consequence of a decision, the more important that decision is.

Okay, so now you know the principles of good decision-making. But the final part of the process is acting—actually making the ethical choice. Most of us know—most of the time—what the ethical choice is. The question is whether we *do it*—even if the consequences are costly to us or to others we care about.

Decision-Making Helpers

Choices are not always clear. Sometimes you will be pulled in many different directions as you consider what to do. Here are a few questions to ask yourself as you consider a decision. The answers may help to make the right choice clearer.

1. **Ask Yourself the Question of Universality**: If everyone made this choice, would it be a good thing?

2. **Ask Yourself the Golden Rule Question**: Would you want someone else to make this choice if it affected you the same way?

3. **Ask Yourself the Role Model Question**: Think of someone you know who is ethical and of strong character. What would that person do?

Tiger Woods is considered by many to be one of the best role models in sports.

Building character is a lifelong process that takes courage, persistence, and strength.

Ethics Is Not for Wimps

Remember, being ethical is not always easy. It takes strength. And it often takes courage.

Being a person of strong character is not something that happens in a day or a week, or even years. For most "mere mortals," the strengthening of character is a lifelong process. There are always things to improve. Every year you work at it, your character will get better and better.

Ethical decisions can be difficult to make—and even more difficult to act upon. But great satisfaction and self-esteem come with knowing you did the right thing. Those positive feelings will inspire you to always make the right choices. This kind of satisfaction lasts a lifetime and brings you the most rewarding feeling of all: happiness.

Resources

WEB SITE:

CharacterCounts.org: The official site of CHARACTER COUNTS! provides information on programs, offers free resources and materials for students, parents, and teachers; also includes links to many other valuable and related sites.

NOTABLE BOOKS ABOUT FAIRNESS:

Firegold by Dia Calhoun: published by Farrar, Straus and Giroux; Sunburst edition, 2003)

The Janitor's Boy by by Andrew Clements and Brian Selznick: published by Aladdin, 2001.

The View from Saturday by E.L. Konigsburg: published by Aladdin, 1998. Newberry Medal Winner.

Jackie's Nine: Jackie Robinson's Values to Live By by Sharon Robinson: published by Scholastic, 2002.

Serving on a Jury by Sarah De Capua: published by Children's Press, 2002.

Glossary

Ethics: guidelines about right and wrong

Impartiality: not having a preference for an outcome

Integrity: knowing and acting on what is right

Stakeholders: people affected by a decision

Segregation: separating people by race

Seniority: preference for those who have served or worked the longest

Suffrage: the right to vote

Universality: applied to everyone

Verdict: legal decision

Voir dire: the process of selecting a jury

Index

Photo Credits